User guide to Mastering your iphone 15 pro

A comprehensive User manual for unlocking the full potential of your apple 15 pro with step by step Tips,Tricks and expert insights

Jackson knight

Table of contents

Chapter 1: Introduction

Welcome to the amazing world of the iPhone 15 Pro! This chapter is all about getting to know your new gadget and setting the stage for an incredible journey. We won't just walk you through the basics; we'll explore the evolution of iPhones, take a peek inside your iPhone 15 Pro, and even touch on the green side of things—how your device is made with the planet in mind.

Getting to Know Your iPhone 15 Pro

Let's start with the basics. Your iPhone 15 Pro isn't just a phone; it's a piece of technology crafted with care. Feel the smoothness of its design and notice the attention to detail. Apple believes in making things not just functional but also beautiful, and your iPhone 15 Pro is a testament to that.

Unboxing and Setting Up

Now, let's dive into the excitement of unboxing your iPhone 15 Pro. What's inside that sleek box matters! From the charging cable to any bonus accessories, each item contributes to your overall experience. And setting up your device is like giving it a passport to your world—we'll guide you step by step.

Evolution of iPhones

It's not just a phone; it's a part of a legacy. iPhones have come a long way, and we're here to take you on a trip through their transformation. From the early models that kickstarted it all to the innovative features packed into the iPhone 15 Pro, see how each step has brought us to this incredible moment.

What Powers Your iPhone 15 Pro

Ever wondered what's under the hood of your iPhone 15 Pro? It's not magic; it's some seriously cool tech. We'll chat about the powerful brain (processor), the stunning display, and the magic behind the camera. Understanding these elements will give you a whole new appreciation for your device.

Your iPhone and the Environment

Now, let's talk about something really important—how your iPhone 15 Pro is a friend to the environment. Apple is committed to sustainability, and your device is designed with eco-friendly initiatives in mind. Knowing that your gadget is made with care for the planet adds an extra layer of pride to owning an iPhone.

Making Your iPhone Uniquely Yours

Your iPhone is not just a gadget; it's an extension of you. We'll dive into the fun part—customization! Learn how to change the look of your home screen, pick cool wallpapers, and make your iPhone 15 Pro reflect your personality. Because why have a phone that looks like everyone else's when yours can be as unique as you are?

Joining the iPhone Community

Your iPhone is part of a big family, and we'll show you how to connect with other iPhone users. From online forums to official support, you're never alone in this journey. Your iPhone has a whole community ready to share tips, tricks, and sometimes just chat about the cool things you can do.

Wrapping Up the Introduction

As we wrap up this introduction, you've not only set up your iPhone 15 Pro but gained insights into its history, inner workings, and the personalization options that await you. You're not just an iPhone owner; you're part of a legacy. Now, let's dive into the fun stuff—what your iPhone 15 Pro can do to make your life more exciting and convenient. Get ready for the adventure ahead!

Chapter 2: Getting Started

Now that your iPhone 15 Pro is out of the box and set up, let's jump into the exciting part—using it! This chapter is like the beginner's guide to your iPhone, helping you navigate, customize, and make the most out of your device. No tech jargon here, just simple steps to get you started.

Navigating the Interface

Alright, let's talk about how to move around your iPhone. It's like your phone's dance floor! You tap to open things, swipe to move around, and press the home button to get back to where you started. We'll walk you through these basic moves so you can navigate your iPhone like a pro, even if it's your first time on the floor.

Customizing Your Home Screen

Think of your home screen like your room—you want it to look and feel just right. We'll show you how to arrange your apps, create folders (they're like little baskets for your apps), and pick a wallpaper that makes you smile. By the end, your home screen will be as unique as you are.

Managing Apps and Widgets

Apps are like your pals—they make your iPhone fun and useful. We'll guide you on how to add new apps, organize them so you can find them easily, and get rid of the ones you don't need anymore. And guess what? Widgets are like mini-apps that give you quick info at a glance. We'll show you how to customize your home screen with these handy little tools.

Face ID and Security

Now, let's talk about security. Your iPhone 15 Pro is like a fortress, and Face ID is the gatekeeper. We'll guide you through setting up Face ID, so only you can unlock your phone with just a glance. It's like magic, but cooler because it keeps your personal stuff safe and sound.

Siri: Your Virtual Assistant

Meet Siri, your virtual helper. She's like a personal assistant living inside your phone. Need to set a reminder? Ask Siri. Curious about the weather? Ask Siri. We'll walk you through talking to Siri and setting her up to understand you better. It's like having a little buddy in your phone always ready to help.

Quick Settings and Control Center

Swipe down, and voila! You've found the Control Center. It's like a secret menu for quick settings. Want to adjust your screen brightness? Toggle Wi-Fi on or off? The Control Center has your back. We'll guide you through this magical place, making your most-used settings just a swipe away.

By the end of this chapter, you'll be tapping, swiping, and talking to your iPhone like a pro. Your home screen will be a reflection of you, and you'll have your own virtual assistant and quick settings at your fingertips. The basics are down, and the fun is just beginning. So, get ready to make your iPhone 15 Pro truly yours and explore what this fantastic device can do for you!

Chapter 3: Essential Features

Now that you've familiarized yourself with the basics, it's time to dive deeper into the essential features that make your iPhone 15 Pro a powerhouse of functionality. In this chapter, we'll explore Face ID and security, Siri as your virtual assistant, and the convenient Quick Settings and Control Center.

Face ID and Security

Imagine your iPhone recognizing you with just a glance—well, that's the magic of Face ID. It's not just a cool feature; it's your phone's way of ensuring that it's really you unlocking it. Setting up Face ID is like teaching your phone to recognize your face. Go to Settings, tap Face ID & Passcode, and follow the simple steps.

Once set up, your iPhone uses the power of facial recognition technology to unlock with a mere look. It's like having a secret handshake with your phone, making sure only you have access to your personal space. Face ID also works with apps, so you can breeze through transactions and logins securely.

Think of Face ID as your phone's guardian, adding an extra layer of security to keep your information safe. And the best part? It's effortless—no need to remember passwords; your face is the key.

Siri: Your Virtual Assistant

Now, let's chat about Siri—your virtual assistant on standby, ready to make your life easier. Think of Siri as your helpful sidekick, always there to lend a hand. You can summon

Siri by saying, "Hey Siri," and then ask her to do various tasks.

Need a reminder for your friend's birthday? Ask Siri. Curious about the weather tomorrow? Ask Siri. She's like your go-to friend who always has the answers. And the more you interact with her, the better she understands your preferences and habits.

Customizing Siri is easy too. Go to Settings, tap Siri & Search, and explore the options. You can teach Siri to pronounce your name correctly, choose your preferred language, and even adjust her voice. It's like having your own personal assistant tailored to your liking.

Quick Settings and Control Center

Swipe down from the top right of your screen, and you'll find the Control Center—a handy hub for quick settings. Adjusting brightness, turning on airplane mode, or toggling Wi-Fi can be done with a simple swipe and tap.

The Control Center is like a shortcut to the essential functions you use daily. Need to activate the flashlight in a dark room? The Control Center has you covered. It's like having a dashboard for your iPhone, giving you quick access to the features you need in the moment.

Customizing the Control Center is a breeze too. Go to Settings, tap Control Center, and personalize the shortcuts. You can add or remove buttons, ensuring that the Control Center caters to your specific needs.

In a nutshell, the Control Center is your command center, putting the most-used settings at your fingertips. It's a time-saver and a game-changer, making your iPhone experience more seamless and efficient.

By the end of this chapter, you've not only mastered the art of unlocking your iPhone with Face ID but also befriended Siri, your virtual assistant, and explored the convenience of the Quick Settings and Control Center. These essential features are the building blocks of a more personalized and efficient iPhone experience. Get ready to take your iPhone 15 Pro skills to the next level in the upcoming chapters!

Chapter 4: Communication

Now that you've become well-acquainted with the foundational features of your iPhone 15 Pro, let's dive into the exciting realm of communication. In this chapter, we'll explore making calls and sending messages, experiencing FaceTime and video calls, and seamlessly integrating email and social media into your iPhone experience.

Making Calls and Sending Messages

Your iPhone is not just a high-tech gadget; it's a communication powerhouse. Making calls is as simple as tapping the phone icon and selecting a contact. Need to send a quick message? The Messages app is your go-to. It's like having your own personal communication hub.

Explore the world of contacts by adding favorites for those you reach out to most frequently. It's like creating a speed dial for your favorite people. You can also customize contacts with photos, making your calls and messages more visually engaging.

Group messages are another fun feature. Create a group for family, friends, or work, and stay connected with everyone in one thread. It's like having a virtual hangout where you can share updates, plans, and inside jokes.

FaceTime and Video Calls

In the era of visual communication, FaceTime is your ticket to face-to-face interactions, even if you're miles apart. It's like bringing people into your world with just a tap.

Start a FaceTime call with a friend or family member and see their smiling face in real time.

Video calls are not just limited to FaceTime. With various messaging apps available, you can connect with friends using video calls on platforms like WhatsApp or Zoom. It's like having a virtual meeting space right in your pocket.

Explore the joy of video communication—whether it's sharing a moment, celebrating an occasion, or simply catching up, video calls add a personal touch to your connections.

Email and Social Media Integration

Your iPhone is not just about calls and texts; it's your gateway to the digital world.

Email integration is seamless, with the Mail app providing easy access to your emails. Set up your accounts, and you'll receive notifications whenever a new message arrives. It's just like you having your mailbox in your pocket.

Social media enthusiasts, rejoice! Your favorite platforms are just a tap away. Whether it's Facebook, Instagram, Twitter, or others, the social media apps on your iPhone allow you to stay connected, share updates, and engage with your online community. It's like having a front-row seat to the digital social scene.

Additionally, take advantage of widgets on your home screen to get a glimpse of recent emails, messages, or social media updates without opening the apps. It's like having a personalized dashboard for your digital communication.

Customizing notifications ensures that you stay in the loop without feeling overwhelmed. Manage your preferences in Settings, and tailor notifications to suit your communication style. It's like having your iPhone understand when to grab your attention and when to let you focus.

By the end of this chapter, you've not only mastered the art of making calls and sending messages but also experienced the joy of FaceTime and video calls. Plus, you've seamlessly integrated email and social media into your iPhone routine, making communication a breeze. Get ready to explore even more features as we venture into the multimedia experience in the upcoming chapters!

Chapter 5: Multimedia Experience

Welcome to the vibrant world of multimedia with your iPhone 15 Pro! This chapter is all about capturing stunning photos and videos, editing and organizing your media, and immersing yourself in the world of Apple Music and Podcasts.

Capturing Stunning Photos and Videos

Your iPhone 15 Pro is equipped with an impressive camera system that turns every moment into a visual masterpiece. The Camera app is your gateway to creativity, offering various modes and features to capture the perfect shot.

Experiment with different shooting modes like Photo, Portrait, and Night mode. It's like having a versatile tool for every lighting condition. Use Portrait mode to add a professional touch to your photos, creating a beautiful blur in the background that makes your subject stand out.

Don't forget about Live Photos—a feature that captures a few seconds of movement before and after the photo. It's like freezing a moment in time with a touch of life. Explore the possibilities of capturing movement, laughter, or a spontaneous gesture in each shot.

For videos, the Camera app allows you to shoot in different resolutions and frame rates. Whether you're recording a family event or a scenic landscape, your iPhone empowers you to become a storyteller through videos.

Editing and Organizing Media

Once you've captured your media, the fun continues with editing and organization. The Photos app is your virtual darkroom, offering a range of editing tools to enhance your photos.

Crop and rotate to focus on the essentials, adjust brightness and contrast to fine-tune the exposure, and apply filters for an artistic touch. It's like having a photo studio in the palm of your hand. The app also allows you to organize your photos into albums, creating a visual diary of your memories.

Explore the Memories feature that automatically curates collections of your photos and videos based on events, people, or places. It's like having a personal storyteller that brings your memories to life. Customize your memories by adding music, adjusting the duration, and selecting highlight photos.

For video editing, iMovie is your creative suite. Trim clips, add transitions, and include music to create your cinematic masterpiece. It's like being the director of your own movie, and the intuitive interface makes it easy for beginners to dive into video editing.

Exploring Apple Music and Podcast

Your iPhone 15 Pro isn't just a camera; it's also your portable entertainment center. Apple Music offers a vast library of songs, playlists, and artists, providing the soundtrack to your life. Create playlists for different moods or activities, and discover new music through curated recommendations. It's like having a personal DJ that understands your taste.

Podcasts, on the other hand, open the door to a world of audio storytelling. From informative discussions to captivating narratives, the Podcasts app allows you to explore a diverse range of topics. Subscribe to your favorite shows, and listen during your commute, workout, or relaxation time. It's like having a radio station tailored to your interests.

Take advantage of the Music and Podcasts widgets on your home screen to have quick access to your latest tunes and episodes. It's like having a personalized radio station and podcast station at your fingertips.

Creating Memories with Shared Albums

In addition to organizing your media individually, Shared Albums in the Photos app enable you to create collaborative spaces for memories. It's like having a virtual photo album that friends and family can contribute to. Create an album for a special event, share the link, and let others add their photos and videos. It's a collective experience that turns memories into shared stories.

Augmented Reality (AR) Experiences

Your iPhone 15 Pro introduces you to the world of augmented reality (AR), adding a layer of virtual experiences to your real-world surroundings. Explore AR apps that bring learning, gaming, and creativity to a whole new level. It's like stepping into a world where the digital and physical seamlessly blend.

With AR, you can measure objects, visualize furniture in your space before buying, or even engage in interactive gaming experiences. The possibilities are vast, and the App Store offers a variety of AR apps catering to different interests and preferences.

By the end of this chapter, you've not only unleashed your creativity in capturing stunning photos and videos but also mastered the art of editing and organizing your media. Additionally, you've explored the realms of Apple Music and Podcasts, transforming your iPhone 15 Pro into a versatile multimedia powerhouse. Get ready to delve even deeper into the advanced functionalities and productivity features in the chapters that follow!

Chapter 6: Advanced Functionalities

Welcome to the realm of advanced functionalities on your iPhone 15 Pro! This chapter will take you beyond the basics, exploring features that enhance productivity, streamline tasks, and unlock the full potential of your device. Get ready to delve into the world of widgets, shortcuts, and advanced settings.

Widgets for Productivity

Widgets are like little information nuggets that reside on your home screen, providing quick access to essential updates without opening apps. Your iPhone 15 Pro introduces an enhanced widget experience, allowing you to customize and organize your home screen for maximum efficiency.

Explore widgets for weather updates, calendar events, news headlines, and more. These bite-sized previews keep you informed at a glance, streamlining your daily routine. To add a widget, tap and hold on an empty space on your home screen, then click the "+" icon in the top left corner. It's like tailoring your iPhone to display the information that matters most to you.

Shortcuts for Streamlined Tasks

Shortcuts are your personal automation assistant, allowing you to create customized sequences of actions that can be triggered by a single tap. The Shortcuts app on your iPhone empowers you to automate routine tasks, making your device work smarter for you.

For example, create a shortcut that sends a pre-written message to a specified contact with just one tap. Or set up a shortcut to turn on specific settings, like activating Do Not Disturb during work hours. It's like having a digital assistant that anticipates your needs and executes tasks on your behalf.

To get started with Shortcuts, open the Shortcuts app on your iPhone. Tap the "+" icon to create a new shortcut, add actions, and customize the sequence to fit your preferences. Shortcuts bring efficiency to your fingertips, simplifying complex tasks with a single tap.

Advanced Settings for Personalization

Your iPhone 15 Pro is all about personalization, and diving into advanced settings allows you to tailor your device to your unique preferences. Explore settings that go beyond the basics, offering a deeper level of control and customization.

For example, fine-tune your privacy settings by managing app permissions and location services. It's like putting you in the driver's seat, deciding when and how your iPhone shares information. Additionally, explore accessibility settings that cater to specific needs, such as larger text, voice control, or color adjustments.

In the Display & Brightness settings, you can adjust the text size, choose between light and dark mode, and even enable True Tone for a more comfortable viewing experience. It's like having a device that adapts to your environment and preferences.

- ## Gestures for Effortless Navigation

Your iPhone 15 Pro introduces a range of intuitive gestures that enhance your navigation experience. Mastering these gestures allows you to interact with your device seamlessly, without the need for physical buttons.

For instance, swipe up from the bottom to return to the home screen, or swipe down from the top-right corner for the Control Center. These gestures make navigation feel natural, like an extension of your movements.

Explore the multitasking gesture by swiping left or right on the bottom edge of the screen. It's like flipping through different pages of your digital world effortlessly. These gestures add a layer of fluidity to your interactions, making your iPhone a joy to use.

iCloud for Seamless Synchronization

iCloud is your digital cloud companion, ensuring seamless synchronization of your data across all your Apple devices. Whether it's photos, contacts, or documents, iCloud keeps everything up to date, making your iPhone 15 Pro an integral part of your Apple ecosystem.

Activate iCloud in the settings, and choose the data you want to sync. It's like having a personal assistant that ensures your information is always in sync, no matter which Apple device you're using. iCloud is the bridge that connects your iPhone to your iPad, Mac, and other Apple devices, creating a unified and interconnected experience.

App Library for Organized Access

The App Library is your iPhone's way of decluttering and organizing your apps automatically. It's like a digital library that categorizes your apps, making it easier for you to find what you need.

Access the App Library by swiping to the left on your home screen. Apps are grouped into categories like Social, Productivity, and Entertainment. It's like having a personal librarian that knows where every app belongs, saving you time and effort in searching.

Customize your home screen by hiding app pages, keeping only the essentials visible. It's like arranging your digital space to suit your preferences, creating a clutter-free and organized environment.

By exploring these advanced functionalities, you're unlocking the true potential of your iPhone 15 Pro. Widgets and shortcuts streamline your tasks, advanced settings offer personalized control, gestures make navigation effortless, iCloud ensures seamless synchronization, and the App Library declutters your digital space. Get ready to maximize your iPhone experience and discover even more features in the chapters that follow!

Chapter 7: Enhanced Security and Privacy

In this chapter, we'll delve into the robust security and privacy features of your iPhone 15 Pro, ensuring that your personal data remains protected and your digital experience is secure. From biometric authentication to app permissions, Apple prioritizes your privacy. Let's explore the tools and settings that put you in control.

Face ID and Touch ID: Your Digital Gatekeepers

Face ID and Touch ID are like the guardians of your digital fortress, providing secure and convenient methods for unlocking your iPhone, authorizing app transactions, and ensuring that only you have access to sensitive information.

With Face ID, your iPhone uses facial recognition technology to authenticate your identity. It's like a digital key that unlocks your device with just a glance. Set up Face ID in the settings, and your iPhone becomes uniquely yours, recognizing your face securely and efficiently.

For those who prefer a tactile approach, Touch ID is your fingerprint-based authentication system. It's like having a secret handshake with your device. Register your fingerprint in the settings, and effortlessly unlock your iPhone or authorize app purchases with a touch.

App Permissions: Your Control Center

Your iPhone 15 Pro gives you control over how apps access your data. App permissions are like gatekeepers, allowing you to decide what information each app can use. Navigate to Settings, then select an app to customize its permissions.

For example, if a photo-editing app requests access to your camera, you can grant or deny permission. It's just like when having the power to decide which doors are open and which door remains closed. Review app permissions regularly to ensure that your privacy preferences align with your usage.

Location Services: Your Location, Your Choice*

Location Services on your iPhone enhance the functionality of various apps, providing location-specific information. However, you're in control of when and how your location is shared. Head to Settings, tap Privacy, and then Location Services to manage your preferences.

You can choose whether an app gets access to your location always, only when the app is in use, or never. It's like having a map where you decide when to drop a pin and when to keep your location hidden. This level of control ensures that your movements are on your terms.

Safari Privacy Features: Your Browsing Shield*

Safari, your default web browser, comes equipped with privacy features that shield your online activity. Intelligent Tracking Prevention (ITP) is like your digital bodyguard, blocking unwanted trackers from monitoring your browsing behavior.

Additionally, Safari offers a Privacy Report that provides insights into how websites handle your privacy. It's like having a personal detective that keeps you informed about the websites you visit. Access the Privacy Report by tapping the double-A icon in the address bar.

Private Relay: Your Virtual Privacy Shield

Private Relay, a feature introduced with iCloud+, takes your online privacy to the next level. It's like having a virtual privacy shield for your internet connection. Private Relay ensures that your browsing activity remains encrypted and private, even from your internet service provider.

Enable Private Relay in the iCloud settings, and your data gets an extra layer of protection as it travels between your device and the internet. It's like sending your data through a secure tunnel, shielding it from prying eyes and enhancing your online privacy.

App Tracking Transparency: Your Ad Blocker*

Your iPhone 15 Pro introduces App Tracking Transparency, giving you the power to control how apps track your activity across other companies' apps and websites. It's like having an ad blocker for your digital footprint.

When an app wants to track you, it now needs your explicit permission. You'll receive a prompt asking if you want to allow the app to track your activity. It's like deciding who gets the key to your personal information. This transparency ensures that you are aware of and in control of the data you share.

Intelligent Suggestions: Your Smart Assistant*

Your iPhone is designed to be a smart assistant that respects your privacy. Intelligent Suggestions provide personalized recommendations without compromising your data. For instance, the keyboard suggests words based on your typing style, but this data is processed on your device without being sent to Apple servers.

It's like having a helpful assistant that knows your preferences without having to know the details. Enjoy personalized suggestions while maintaining the privacy of your keyst

Chapter 8: Accessibility and Inclusivity

Your iPhone 15 Pro is designed to be inclusive, ensuring that everyone, regardless of abilities or preferences, can have a seamless and enjoyable experience. In this chapter, we'll explore the accessibility features that make your device adaptable to various needs, from visual and auditory assistance to touch and motor skill support.

VoiceOver: Your Digital Narrator

VoiceOver is your digital narrator, providing spoken descriptions of what's happening on your iPhone. It's like having a guide that reads out loud the elements on your screen, making it accessible for those with visual impairments.

To activate VoiceOver, go to Settings, tap Accessibility, then VoiceOver. Once enabled, your iPhone will audibly describe items, text, and even touch gestures, ensuring that users with visual impairments can navigate their device with confidence.

Magnifier: Your Portable Magnifying Glass

The Magnifier feature turns your iPhone into a portable magnifying glass, assisting those with low vision. Activate Magnifier by triple-pressing the side or home button (depending on your device model) or by adding it to your Control Center.

Magnifier allows you to zoom in on text, objects, or anything you need a closer look at. It's like having a magnifying glass that fits right in your pocket, enhancing the visual experience for users with low vision.

Hearing Aid Compatibility: Your Clear Connection*

Your iPhone is designed with hearing aid compatibility, ensuring clear audio for users with hearing aids or cochlear implants. The "Made for iPhone" hearing aids seamlessly connect to your device, providing a direct and customizable audio experience.

To check compatibility and pair your hearing aids, go to Settings, tap Accessibility, then Hearing Devices. It's like having a tailored audio solution that caters to individual hearing needs, promoting inclusivity for users with hearing impairments.

Sound Recognition: Your Alert Listener

Sound Recognition is your alert listener, notifying you of important environmental sounds. It's like having a digital ear that can detect alarms, sirens, doorbells, and more. This feature is particularly beneficial for users with hearing impairments, adding an extra layer of awareness to their surroundings.

To enable Sound Recognition, go to Settings, tap Accessibility, then Sound Recognition. Customize the sounds you want to be notified about, and your iPhone will alert you when they are detected.

AssistiveTouch: Your Custom Controls

AssistiveTouch is your customizable control center, providing an alternative for users with motor skill challenges. It's like having a set of virtual buttons and gestures that make navigation more accessible.

Activate AssistiveTouch in Settings under Accessibility, and you'll see a menu of touch gestures and controls on your screen. Customize these controls based on your preferences, creating shortcuts for actions like taking screenshots, adjusting volume, or accessing the home screen.

Switch Control: Your Adaptive Input

Switch Control is an adaptive input method for users with limited mobility. It's like having a customizable switch interface that enables you to control your iPhone using external switches or the device's screen.

To set up Switch Control, go to Settings, tap Accessibility, then Switch Control. Customize the switches and gestures to match your needs, providing an accessible way to interact with your device.

Voice Control transforms your spoken words into device commands, offering an alternative input method for users with mobility challenges. It's like having a vocal command center that allows you to navigate, open apps, and perform various tasks using your voice.

Activate Voice Control in Settings under Accessibility, then Voice Control. Once enabled, you can use natural language commands to control your iPhone. It's a hands-free solution that promotes accessibility and inclusivity.

Inclusive Design: Your User-Centric Approach

Beyond individual features, Apple follows a philosophy of inclusive design, considering diverse needs and preferences from the initial design stages. It's like having a user-centric approach that values accessibility as an integral part of the overall user experience.

From the carefully selected color palettes to the intuitive gestures, Apple aims to create products that are accessible to everyone. This commitment to inclusive design ensures that users of all abilities can benefit from the technological advancements of the iPhone 15 Pro.

In conclusion, your iPhone 15 Pro is not just a device; it's a platform for inclusivity and accessibility. Features like VoiceOver, Magnifier, and Sound Recognition cater to specific needs, while AssistiveTouch, Switch Control, and Voice Control offer adaptive input methods. The commitment to inclusive design ensures that your iPhone is accessible to users with diverse abilities, fostering a digital environment where everyone can participate fully and enjoy the benefits of technology.

Chapter 9: Digital Wellbeing

In an era dominated by technology, maintaining a healthy relationship with your iPhone 15 Pro is crucial. This chapter delves into the digital wellbeing features designed to help you strike a balance between your online and offline life, promoting mindfulness, and fostering a healthy relationship with technology.

Screen Time: Your Digital Hourglas

Screen Time is like your digital hourglass, providing insights into how much time you spend on your device and specific apps. It's not about limiting your usage but empowering you with information to make conscious choices.

To access Screen Time, go to Settings, tap Screen Time. Here, you'll find a breakdown of your daily and weekly activities, app usage patterns, and even insights into notifications. Set daily limits for app categories or individual apps, and your iPhone will remind you when you're approaching your predefined usage thresholds.

App Limits: Your Time Boundaries

Building on Screen Time, App Limits allow you to set specific time boundaries for app categories. It's like having a gentle reminder that encourages you to balance your digital engagements.

If social media tends to take up more time than you'd like, set an App Limit for that category. When your allocated time is about to expire, your iPhone notifies you. It's a helpful tool for creating mindful usage habits without completely cutting off access to your favorite apps.

Downtime: Your Digital Sabbath

Downtime is your digital sabbath, a designated period when only essential apps and phone calls are accessible. It's like carving out intentional breaks from constant connectivity.

Specify your Downtime hours in Screen Time settings, and during these periods, non-essential apps will be grayed out on your home screen. This feature encourages you to unwind, focus on other activities, and establish a healthier balance between your digital and real-world experiences.

Wind Down: Your Tech-Free Transition to Sleep

Quality sleep is essential for overall wellbeing. Wind Down is your tech-free transition to a good night's sleep. It's like having a gentle prompt to prepare for bedtime without the distractions of notifications and bright screens.

Configure Wind Down in the Health app under Sleep, and your iPhone will create a calming routine leading up to your bedtime. Dimming the screen, activating Do Not Disturb, and displaying a personalized sleep summary help you unwind and establish healthy sleep habits.

Grayscale: Your Distraction Dimmer

Grayscale is your distraction dimmer, turning your iPhone screen monochromatic. It's like seeing the digital world in black and white, reducing the visual appeal of colorful apps and potentially curbing excessive usage.

To enable Grayscale, go to Settings, tap Accessibility, then Display & Text Size. Activate the Color Filters option and select Grayscale. While it might seem subtle, the change can contribute to a less visually stimulating experience, especially during times when you aim to minimize distractions.

App Library Organization: Your Clutter Cutter

App Library is not just about decluttering; it's your tool for organized access. It's like having a minimalist approach to your home screen, prioritizing what matters most.

Swiping left from your main home screen reveals the App Library, where apps are categorized automatically. By reducing the visual noise on your home screen, you can enhance focus and minimize the temptation to mindlessly scroll through apps.

Focus: Your Tailored Distraction Filters

Focus is your tailored distraction filter, allowing you to customize notification preferences based on your current activity or mindset. It's like having a dynamic notification assistant that understands when you need to concentrate and when you're ready to unwind.

Create different Focus modes for activities like work, personal time, or sleep. Each mode can have its own set of allowed notifications, ensuring that your iPhone adapts to your needs. Access Focus in Settings, tap Focus, and customize the modes that suit your lifestyle.

Mindfulness and Breathe: Your Calm Companion

Mindfulness and Breathe are your calm companions, offering guided sessions to help you relax and practice mindfulness. It's like having a pocket-sized meditation coach that reminds you to take a moment for yourself.

Access the Breathe app or set up Mindfulness reminders in the Health app to incorporate short meditation breaks into your day. These features emphasize the importance of mental wellbeing, encouraging you to pause, breathe, and center yourself amidst the hustle and bustle of daily life.

In conclusion, the digital wellbeing features on your iPhone 15 Pro are not about restricting your usage but empowering you to maintain a healthy relationship with technology. Screen Time, App Limits, Downtime, Wind Down, Grayscale, App Library, Focus, and Mindfulness collectively provide tools for mindful usage, helping you strike a balance between your digital and real-world experiences. Embrace these features to foster a healthier and more intentional interaction with your device.

Chapter 10: Continuous Learning and Productivity

Your iPhone 15 Pro isn't just a device for communication and entertainment; it's a powerful tool for continuous learning and productivity. This chapter explores features and apps that transform your iPhone into a dynamic platform for acquiring new knowledge, staying organized, and boosting your efficiency in various aspects of life.

Books and Audiobooks: Your Portable Library

The Books app on your iPhone is like a portable library, offering access to a vast collection of ebooks and audiobooks. Whether you prefer to read or listen, this app provides a convenient way to dive into literature, expand your knowledge, or enjoy a captivating story.

Browse the Book Store, download your favorite titles, and start reading or listening anytime, anywhere. With features like Night mode for comfortable reading in low light and the ability to adjust text size and font, the Books app caters to your reading preferences.

Notes: Your Digital Notebook

The Notes app on your iPhone is your digital notebook, ready to capture your thoughts, ideas, and important information. It's like having a versatile tool for note-taking, project planning, and organization.

Create checklists, sketches, and text notes effortlessly. Use the powerful search feature to find specific notes quickly. Collaborate with others by sharing notes and syncing them across your Apple devices through iCloud. The simplicity and functionality of the Notes app make it an essential companion for staying organized and boosting productivity.

Calendar: Your Schedule Keeper

The Calendar app is like your personal schedule keeper, helping you stay organized and on top of your commitments. Whether it's meetings, appointments, or events, this app ensures that you never miss a beat.

Create events, set reminders, and color-code your schedule for clarity. The Calendar app integrates seamlessly with other apps, such as Maps and Contacts, making it easy to add locations and invite attendees. Stay organized and manage your time effectively with the Calendar app.

Reminders: Your Task Manager

Reminders is your task manager, ensuring that you stay on top of your to-do list. It's like having a digital assistant that nudges you to complete tasks and accomplish goals.

Create lists for different aspects of your life, set due dates, and receive notifications to keep you on track. The simplicity and flexibility of the Reminders app make it a valuable tool for managing tasks, projects, and daily responsibilities.

News: Your Personal Newsstand

The News app transforms your iPhone into a personal newsstand, delivering curated content tailored to your interests. It's like having a customized newspaper that keeps you informed about the topics you care about.

Explore articles from reputable sources, follow your favorite publications, and discover new perspectives. The News app offers a personalized and efficient way to stay updated on current events, trends, and topics of interest.

Files: Your Mobile File Cabinet

The Files app is like your mobile file cabinet, providing easy access to documents, images, and files stored on your iPhone and in iCloud. It's an essential tool for staying organized and ensuring that your important files are just a tap away.

Organize your files into folders, and use the search feature to quickly locate specific documents. The Files app supports various file types, making it a versatile solution for managing your digital content.

Podcasts: Your On-the-Go Learning Companion

The Podcasts app on your iPhone is like a mobile classroom, offering a wide range of educational content on diverse topics. It's a convenient way to learn on the go, whether you're commuting, exercising, or taking a break.

Subscribe to podcasts that align with your interests and goals. From educational series to expert interviews, the Podcasts app provides valuable insights and knowledge from various fields.

Health: Your Wellness Dashboard

The Health app is your wellness dashboard, consolidating data from various health and fitness apps into one central location. It's like having a comprehensive overview of your health and activity levels.

Track your steps, monitor your sleep, and record other health-related metrics. The Health app allows you to set health goals, view trends over time, and share important health information with healthcare professionals. It's a holistic approach to managing your well-being.

Learn: Your Educational Hub

The Learn app is your educational hub, offering a variety of courses and tutorials to enhance your skills and knowledge. It's like having a virtual classroom where you can explore subjects ranging from language learning to professional development.

Enroll in courses, watch video lessons, and track your progress. The Learn app provides a flexible and accessible way to engage in continuous learning, empowering you to acquire new skills and stay ahead in your personal and professional journey.

Widgets for Productivity: Your Customizable Dashboard

Widgets are your customizable dashboard, providing at-a-glance information and quick access to key apps. It's like having a personalized command center that reflects your priorities and activities.

Add widgets for Calendar events, Reminders, News headlines, and more to your home screen. Widgets offer a dynamic and efficient way to stay informed and organized without having to open multiple apps.

In conclusion, your iPhone 15 Pro is not just a communication device but a versatile tool for continuous learning and productivity. From reading books and managing your schedule to staying informed with news and podcasts, your iPhone empowers you to lead a well-rounded and organized life. Embrace these features and apps to make the most of your digital experience.

Chapter 11: Creative Expression and Multimedia

Your iPhone 15 Pro is a canvas for creative expression and multimedia exploration. In this chapter, we'll unravel the features and apps that transform your device into a powerful tool for capturing, editing, and sharing your visual and auditory experiences.

Camera: Capturing Moments in Style

The Camera app is your gateway to capturing moments in style. With advanced camera technology, including multiple lenses and computational photography, your iPhone 15 Pro transforms every shot into a visual masterpiece.

Explore the various modes such as Photo, Portrait, and Night mode to adapt to different lighting conditions. Capture stunning landscapes, create professional-looking portraits, and take vibrant low-light shots. The Camera app empowers you to express your creativity with just a tap.

Photo Editing: Unleashing Your Inner Artist

Once you've captured your photos, the Photo app invites you to unleash your inner artist through intuitive editing tools. It's like having a virtual darkroom at your fingertips.

Crop and straighten images, adjust brightness and contrast, and apply artistic filters to add a personal touch. Dive into the detailed editing options, such as adjusting individual color levels and enhancing fine details. The Photo app transforms your iPhone into a creative tool for crafting visually stunning images.

iMovie: Cinematic Storytelling Made Easy

iMovie is your cinematic storytelling companion, providing a user-friendly platform for editing videos. It's like having a video editing suite in the palm of your hand.

Trim and arrange clips, add transitions, and incorporate music to create captivating videos. iMovie's intuitive interface makes it accessible to beginners while offering advanced features for those looking to dive deeper into video editing. Express your narrative through moving images with iMovie.

GarageBand turns your iPhone into a pocket-sized music studio, allowing you to create and edit music with ease. It's like having a versatile set of musical instruments and recording tools in your pocket.

Compose original tunes, experiment with various instruments, and record your vocals. GarageBand supports both beginners and experienced musicians, offering features like loops, virtual instruments, and multi-track recording. Whether you're a budding artist or an experienced composer, GarageBand makes music creation accessible to all.

Clips: Expressive Video Messaging

Clips is your tool for expressive video messaging, combining video clips, photos, and music into shareable creations. It's like having a mini-production studio for crafting dynamic and entertaining videos.

Record video snippets, add animated stickers, captions, and soundtracks to enhance your message. Clips is designed for quick and creative video creation, making it an ideal app for sharing memorable moments, announcements, or just expressing yourself in a fun and engaging way.

Procreate Pocket: Artistic Sketching on the Go

Procreate Pocket is your pocket-sized canvas for digital sketching and painting. It's like having a full-fledged art studio in the palm of your hand.

Create intricate illustrations, explore a vast array of brushes and tools, and unleash your artistic vision. Procreate Pocket supports layers, offering advanced features for artists who want to take their digital art to the next level. Express your creativity wherever inspiration strikes with Procreate Pocket.

Music Memos: Capture Your Musical Ideas

For musicians and songwriters, Music Memos is your companion for capturing and organizing musical ideas. It's like having a musical notepad that preserves your melodies and lyrics on the spot.

Record your musical ideas using your iPhone's built-in microphone. Music Memos automatically analyzes the tempo, key, and rhythm, turning your raw recordings into fully realized compositions. Whether you're a professional musician or someone who enjoys creating music as a hobby, Music Memos is a valuable tool for preserving your creative sparks.

AR Experiences: Augmented Reality Unleashed

Augmented Reality (AR) experiences on your iPhone 15 Pro take multimedia exploration to the next level. It's like stepping into a world where the digital and physical seamlessly blend.

Explore AR apps that bring learning, gaming, and interactive experiences to life. Measure objects in your environment, visualize furniture in your space before purchasing, or engage in immersive gaming adventures. The possibilities are vast, and AR apps provide a new dimension to creative expression.

AirPods and Spatial Audio: Immersive Soundscapes

Your iPhone 15 Pro, coupled with AirPods and Spatial Audio, delivers an immersive audio experience. It's like stepping into a three-dimensional soundscape that enhances your listening pleasure.

Spatial Audio provides a dynamic audio experience, adjusting the sound based on your head movements for a lifelike feel. Whether you're listening to music, watching movies, or playing games, AirPods and Spatial Audio create an immersive auditory experience that complements your multimedia adventures.

Memojis and Animojis: Animated Self-Expression

Memojis and Animojis are your animated self-expression tools, allowing you to create personalized animated characters that mimic your facial expressions and movements. It's like having a virtual avatar that brings your messages and FaceTime calls to life.

Create a Memoji that reflects your personality, and use it in Messages, FaceTime, and other apps. Animojis add a playful touch, turning your favorite emojis into animated characters that mirror your own expressions. Express yourself in a whole new way with Memojis and Animojis.

In conclusion, your iPhone 15 Pro is a versatile platform for creative expression and multimedia exploration. From capturing moments with the advanced camera to editing photos and videos, creating music, sketching digital art, and exploring augmented reality, your iPhone empowers you to unleash your creativity in various forms. Embrace these features and apps to turn your device into a dynamic tool for self-expression and multimedia creation.

CONCLUSION

In concluding "Mastering Your iPhone 15 Pro User Guide," I trust this journey through the intricacies of your powerful device has empowered you. From unlocking advanced features to navigating security and privacy settings, this guide aimed to elevate your iPhone experience. May your newfound mastery enhance your daily life, productivity, and creative pursuits. As a dedicated tech professional, my goal has been to provide a comprehensive yet accessible resource, ensuring you harness the full potential of the iPhone 15 Pro.

Thank you for entrusting me as your guide on this technological odyssey. Your support is invaluable. If you found this guide helpful, I encourage you to share your experience with others by leaving a 5-star review. Your feedback fuels the passion for creating insightful content. Here's to mastering your iPhone 15 Pro – may it be a constant companion on your journey through the digital landscape.